EMBRACING TRANQUILITY
DISCOVERING GOD'S PEACE BEYOND BELIEFS

ALAIN LEA

Copyright © 2023 by Alain Lea

All rights reserved. No part of this publication may be reproduced, distributed, or transmitted in any form or by any means, including photocopying, recording, or other electronic or mechanical methods, without the prior written permission of the publisher, except in the case of brief quotations embodied in critical reviews and certain other noncommercial uses permitted by copyright law.

Published by Christ In All Nations Publishing
Granger, Indiana 46530, USA.

Printed in United States Of America

For permission requests, write to the publisher at the address above, or contact: infos@christinallnations.org or www.christinallnations.org

Embracing Tranquility: Discovering God's Peace Beyond Beliefs

Alain Lea
ISBN: 978-1-952806-29-2
1. Spirituality and Faith
2. Conflict Resolution and Peacemaking
3. Personal Growth and Development
4. Mindfulness and Meditation Practices

TABLE OF CONTENTS

Preface v

Introduction vii

CHAPTER ONE

The Meaning of God's Peace: A Heavenly Serenity 3

Finding Peace in God: A Loving Embrace 5

Embracing Peace from God: Trust, Surrender & Faith 7

God's Peace Verses: Insights from the Bible 9

The Benefits of God's Peace: Holistic Harmony 11

Prayers for the Peace of God: Conversations with The Divine 13

Experiencing Inner Peace with God: A Personal Journey 15

God's Peace: A Stronghold in Hard Times 17

Mental Peace Through God: The Ultimate Solace 19

God's Peace vs World's Peace: A Stark Contrast 21

Maintaining God's Peace: Sustaining Spiritual Serenity 23

CHAPTER TWO

Experiencing God's Incomprehensible Peace 27

Embracing the Inexplicable 29

Surrendering to the Ineffable 32

Embracing God's Unfathomable Gift 33

Conclusion: Cultivating the Culture of Peace 34

FAQs 36

Appendix 45

The Ultimate Invitation 50

About The Author 52

PREFACE

In a world often marked by division, chaos, and the relentless pursuit of solace, the concept of peace becomes a universal yearning—a whisper amid the clamor of our existence. We seek it in our relationships, our endeavors, and within the depths of our souls. Yet, peace seems elusive, a fleeting mirage in the desert of life's uncertainties.

This book, "Embracing Tranquility: Discovering God's Peace Beyond Beliefs," emerges as a guiding light amidst this quest for peace—a journey not confined by the boundaries of faith or the limitations of religious doctrines. Instead, it's an exploration of a profound truth—that God's peace transcends the confines of religious structures, embracing every seeking heart, regardless of background or beliefs.

In these pages, we embark on a pilgrimage—a pilgrimage not confined to holy sites or sacred texts, but one that traverses the landscapes of diverse human experiences. It's an odyssey woven with narratives of individuals from various walks of life, each seeking the same elusive tranquility—a peace that quells the storms within, regardless of cultural affiliations, spiritual leanings, or religious convictions.

We delve into the essence of God's peace—a peace that surpasses worldly understanding, that stands as an unwavering sanctuary amid life's turbulence. It's a peace that doesn't merely calm the external storms but anchors the soul in the face of uncertainties, a peace that whispers hope when the world screams chaos.

This book isn't a doctrinal thesis or a theological discourse. It's an embrace—a gesture of inclusivity, inviting seekers and skeptics, believers and doubters, to partake in the profound revelation of a peace that transcends human limitations.

Through the pages that follow, we witness the beauty of diversity—diversity in beliefs, experiences, and perspectives—interwoven to unravel a universal truth: that God's peace is not an exclusive possession but an open invitation to every seeking heart.

May this book serve as a compass guiding you through the labyrinth of life's complexities, illuminating the path toward an all-encompassing peace—a peace that awaits, beckoning each soul to embrace its divine tranquility.

As we embark on this journey together, may the wisdom shared within these pages unveil the beauty of God's peace, uniting us in a shared quest for the profound solace that transcends boundaries and echoes in every seeking heart.

— Alain Lea

INTRODUCTION

Seeking peace is a universal longing, an innate desire woven into the fabric of our existence. We yearn for a tranquility that soothes the clamor of our hectic lives, a respite from the chaos that surrounds us. However, the peace we often chase remains elusive, subject to the whims of external circumstances and fleeting in its presence. It's a fragile state, easily disrupted by the tumult of the world.

Yet, beyond the transient peace we seek, there exists a profound and unwavering serenity—the Peace of God. This divine tranquility transcends human understanding, offering an enduring refuge even amidst the storms of life. Rooted in profound trust and faith, it becomes an anchor for the soul, providing solace that surpasses the turmoil of the external world.

This transcendent peace is reminiscent of the promise Jesus imparted to His followers, a promise that resonates through time and circumstance: "Peace I leave with you; my peace I give you" (John 14:27). It's a peace that surpasses mere absence of conflict—it's a deep-seated assurance, a sense of harmony that resides within, regardless of the chaos that may swirl outside.

The pursuit of this divine peace involves a journey inward, a quest to cultivate faith, trust, and surrender—to allow oneself to be enveloped by a peace that is not contingent upon external conditions. It's a realization that amidst life's upheavals and uncertainties, there remains an unshakable sanctuary within—the Peace of God—that can be accessed through faith and a connection beyond the temporal realm.

In this pursuit, one discovers that true peace isn't merely the absence of chaos but rather an inner sanctuary that remains steadfast even amid life's storms—a sanctuary offered by a higher power, inviting us to experience a tranquility that surpasses all understanding.

    Embracing Tranquility: Discovering God's Peace Beyond Beliefs...

CHAPTER ONE

THE MEANING OF GOD'S PEACE

A HEAVENLY SERENITY

God's Peace, often described in the scriptures as 'shalom,' encompasses far more than the absence of conflict; it represents a state of profound wholeness and completeness rooted in a deep relationship with the divine. It transcends the limitations of worldly understanding, offering a tranquility that reaches into the core of one's being, soothing the soul and bringing a sense of harmony and abundance.

In the Bible, the concept of shalom is layered with significance, portraying a peace that surpasses mere quietness or lack of strife. It embodies a holistic well-being—a state where every aspect of life finds completeness and soundness. It's a tranquility that goes beyond fleeting circumstances, steadying the mind and heart even in the face of turmoil.

The Peace of God functions as a profound anchor in the lives of believers, providing a sense of assurance and confidence in the midst of life's trials. It's the kind of peace that allows one to declare, even in the most challenging times, "It is well with my soul." This declaration isn't merely an affirmation of hope; it's a testament to the unshakeable serenity that comes from a deep connection with the divine.

The beauty of God's Peace lies in its encompassing nature. It extends beyond the turmoil of the world, reaching into the innermost recesses of the human spirit, controlling thoughts, calming fears, and offering a sense of completeness that cannot be shaken by external circumstances.

This peace is beautifully captured in the book of Isaiah: "You keep him in perfect peace whose mind is stayed on you because he trusts in you" (Isaiah 26:3). Here, the verse speaks of a peace that arises from trust and unwavering focus on God—a peace that transcends the chaos of the world by anchoring the mind and soul in divine serenity.

Embracing the Peace of God involves surrendering to this divine tranquility, allowing it to permeate every aspect of life. It's an ongoing journey of trust, faith, and spiritual prosperity that brings about a profound sense of completeness and wholeness found only in a relationship with the Creator.

FINDING PEACE IN GOD

A LOVING EMBRACE

*D*iscovering peace in God is not a quest shrouded in mystery; it's a journey open to all who seek a profound, personal connection with their heavenly Father. Jesus extends an open invitation, urging us, "Come to me, all you who are weary and burdened, and I will give you rest" (Matthew 11:28). This promise encapsulates the accessibility of God's peace to anyone willing to embark on this transformative journey.

The pursuit of God's peace commences with a heart humbled and earnest, acknowledging our limitations while recognizing the boundless sufficiency of God. It involves an intimate connection—a reaching out to the divine, seeking solace and rest in His presence.

To find peace in God is to release the grip of control and surrender our lives, fears, and worries into His care. It's a profound act of trust, anchored in the certainty of God's limitless love and perfect wisdom. This surrender isn't a sign of weakness but a courageous step toward embracing the sovereignty of a higher power, even when the mysteries of His ways elude our understanding.

The Scriptures reassure us in Philippians 4:6-7: "Do not be anxious about anything, but in every situation, by prayer and petition, with thanksgiving, present your requests to God. And the peace of God, which transcends all understanding, will guard your hearts and your minds in Christ Jesus." This passage emphasizes the transformative power of surrender and trust in God's peace that surpasses human comprehension.

Trusting God amidst life's uncertainties becomes the cornerstone of this journey. It involves a relinquishing of our need for comprehension, an embrace of His unfathomable plans, and a surrender to His timing. It's an acknowledgment that His ways surpass our finite understanding, yet His intentions are always rooted in love and goodness.

God's peace beckons those who seek refuge from the chaos of the world—a refuge found not in avoidance or escape, but in a deep and unwavering connection with the divine. It's a peace that doesn't eliminate challenges but empowers us to face them with a resilient spirit and an unshakeable trust in the One who holds all things in His hands.

The pathway to experiencing God's peace is paved with humility, trust, and an unwavering faith in His unwavering presence. It's a journey marked by a continual surrender, a relinquishing of our burdens onto the loving shoulders of a God who invites us into His embrace of unending peace.

EMBRACING PEACE FROM GOD
TRUST, SURRENDER & FAITH

At the core of embracing God's peace lies a triumvirate of virtues: trust, surrender, and faith. These three facets interweave to form the very foundation upon which the Peace of God stands. Trusting God requires an unwavering belief in His goodness, sovereignty, and unchanging nature. It's a resolute assurance that despite the chaos around us, He remains steadfast and faithful.

Surrendering to God demands relinquishing our futile attempts to control life's course and embracing His divine plan over our own desires. It's about releasing our grasp on the steering wheel of life and allowing His wisdom to guide our paths. It's not a sign of weakness but an act of courage—a conscious choice to let go and let God.

Faith acts as the adhesive that binds trust and surrender together. It's the conscious decision to believe in God's promises, even when circumstances seem contradictory. Hebrews 11:1 beautifully captures this essence of faith: "Now faith is confidence in what we hope for and assurance about what we do not see." It's the assurance that what God has promised, He will fulfill, even if the present reality doesn't align with it.

When we wholeheartedly trust in God's promises, surrender our lives into His loving care, and cling steadfastly to faith, we unlock the floodgates for His perfect peace to cascade over us. In this surrender and trust, we find echoes of Paul's profound affirmation: "And the peace of God, which surpasses all understanding, will guard your hearts and your minds in Christ Jesus" (Philippians 4:7).

This divine peace is not merely a fleeting emotion or a temporary fix. It's a profound state of tranquility that transcends human comprehension, enveloping our hearts and minds in a protective embrace amidst life's storms. It's a peace that stands guard, shielding us from anxiety and fear, as we rest in the assurance of God's unwavering love and sovereignty.

Embracing God's peace through trust, surrender, and faith isn't a one-time event; it's a continual journey—a deliberate choice we make each day to lean into His grace, allowing His peace to permeate every facet of our lives.

GOD'S PEACE VERSES

INSIGHTS FROM THE BIBLE

*E*xploring God's peace through the verses of Scripture is akin to unraveling a tapestry woven with divine assurances. Within these sacred texts, believers find a tapestry of promises that affirm God's unwavering calmness amidst life's tumultuous storms.

In Psalm 29:11, we encounter a resounding declaration: "The LORD gives strength to His people; the LORD blesses His people with peace." This verse serves as a beacon of hope, assuring us that within God's strength lies the gift of peace—a peace that transcends circumstances, offering solace and serenity to those who seek refuge in Him.

Jesus, in John 16:33, imparts words of enduring comfort to His disciples and to all who follow Him: "I have told you these things, so that in me you may have peace. In this world, you will have trouble. But take heart! I have overcome the world." These profound words serve as a source of encouragement, acknowledging the inevitable challenges of life while offering a steadfast assurance of peace found in Christ. It's a reminder that despite the turmoil of the world, His victory provides a lasting peace that surpasses all understanding.

Throughout the Bible, God's peace is depicted as a foundational aspect of His character—a peace that remains unshaken by the chaos of the world. Isaiah 26:3 beautifully encapsulates this idea: "You will keep in perfect peace those whose minds are steadfast because they trust in you." This verse underscores the correlation between trust and peace, highlighting that unwavering trust in God serves as a gateway to experiencing His perfect peace, a peace that stands firm in the midst of life's uncertainties.

In Philippians 4:6-7, believers are encouraged: "Do not be anxious about anything, but in every situation, by prayer and petition, with thanksgiving, present your requests to God. And the peace of God, which transcends all understanding, will guard your hearts and your minds in Christ Jesus." This passage emphasizes the transformative power of prayer and gratitude in inviting God's peace to stand guard over our hearts and minds, surpassing human comprehension.

God's peace, as depicted in these verses, is not merely an absence of turmoil but a profound presence—a steadfast calmness offered to those who trust in Him, seek His guidance, and anchor their faith in His promises. It's a peace that surpasses the fleeting tranquility of the world, offering a sanctuary of serenity in the embrace of divine love and grace.

THE BENEFITS OF GOD'S PEACE

HOLISTIC HARMONY

*I*mmersing ourselves in God's peace, as mentioned in Philippians 4:7 ("And the peace of God, which transcends all understanding, will guard your hearts and your minds in Christ Jesus"), offers a profound anchoring effect in tumultuous times. This peace acts as an unshakable foundation, allowing our faith to stand firm amidst life's storms (Matthew 7:24-25). It's a steadfast refuge, enabling us to weather the fiercest of trials without faltering in our trust in God's promises.

This divine peace, rooted in God's character (Isaiah 26:3), instills within us an indomitable courage and strength (Joshua 1:9), transforming our perspective on life's uncertainties. Even in the face of adversity, it bestows a serene contentment and unwavering joy, irrespective of external circumstances (John 16:33).

Beyond its spiritual implications, God's peace significantly impacts our mental and emotional well-being. Romans 15:13 mentions how God fills us with joy and peace as we trust in Him, nurturing our resilience and mindfulness. This peace serves as a catalyst for a positive outlook on life, promoting mental clarity and emotional stability (Isaiah 32:17).

Moreover, the influence of God's peace extends to our relationships, guiding us to cultivate harmony and unity (Ephesians 4:3). As peacemakers (Matthew 5:9), we carry this divine peace within us, fostering environments of reconciliation and understanding in our communities. It empowers us to handle conflicts with grace and compassion, paving the way for healing and restoration (Colossians 3:15).

In essence, God's peace, as described in Philippians 4:7, is holistic. It transcends the spiritual realm, permeating our mental, emotional, and relational spheres. This peace, a gift from God Himself, holds the transformative power to bring harmony within ourselves and radiate that harmony into the world around us.

PRAYERS FOR THE PEACE OF GOD
CONVERSATIONS WITH THE DIVINE

Prayers stand as pivotal moments in our spiritual journey, facilitating an intimate communion with God, inviting His peace into every corner of our lives. They serve as the channel through which we lay bare our souls, expressing our uncertainties, and echoing our earnest longing for the comforting tranquility found in His presence.

In the wisdom of the Apostle Paul, we find guidance on prayer-filled living, as he assures believers of its peace-inducing results: "Do not be anxious about anything, but in every situation, by prayer and petition, with thanksgiving, present your requests to God. And the peace of God, which transcends all understanding, will guard your hearts and your minds in Christ Jesus" (Philippians 4:6-7). Paul's words emphasize the transformative power of prayer, highlighting its ability to usher in a peace that goes beyond human comprehension, a peace that serves as a guardian over our hearts and minds.

Through prayer, we embark on a sacred conversation with the Divine—a dialogue where we pour out our hearts, desires, and fears, and learn to listen for the gentle whispers of God's guidance and reassurance. Jesus Himself exemplified the significance of prayer, often withdrawing to commune with His Father in moments of solitude and seeking divine guidance (Luke 5:16).

In the book of Psalms, we witness the psalmist's earnest cries for peace and refuge in God: "In peace I will lie down and sleep, for you alone, LORD, make me dwell in safety" (Psalm 4:8). This verse echoes the sentiment that in surrendering our worries and seeking God's presence, we find a tranquil place of rest and security.

Prayers for peace aren't confined to structured rituals but extend to the moments of our daily lives. They can be whispered in the chaos of the day or expressed in silent yearnings of the heart, acknowledging our dependence on a higher power and opening ourselves to the divine peace that surpasses all understanding.

In these moments of communion with the Divine, our hearts find solace, our minds gain clarity, and our spirits discover refuge in the boundless tranquility offered by God. Through prayers, we foster a deeper connection with the Almighty—a connection that becomes a source of strength and serenity amidst life's trials and tribulations.

EXPERIENCING INNER PEACE WITH GOD

A PERSONAL JOURNEY

Discovering peace within God isn't a distant notion confined to religious teachings; it's an intimate, deeply personal expedition of spiritual revelation, transformation, and evolution. Every believer traverses this path uniquely, encountering God's serenity in diverse ways and experiencing the profound tranquility it bestows upon the soul.

These encounters with God's peace often stem from personal trials, where His faithfulness is unmistakably revealed. In moments of trial, His presence becomes palpable, offering a peace that transcends the chaos, a peace beautifully articulated in Isaiah 41:10: "So do not fear, for I am with you; do not be dismayed, for I am your God. I will strengthen you and help you; I will uphold you with my righteous right hand."

Additionally, these experiences can blossom from moments of solitary reflection—a stillness where the noise of the world fades, allowing the whispers of God's peace to resound within. The psalmist captures this sentiment in Psalm 46:10: "Be still, and know that I am God; I will be exalted among the nations, I will be exalted in the earth."

Nature itself becomes a canvas of divine revelation, inspiring awe and reminding us of the Creator's grandeur and goodness. Romans 1:20 beautifully emphasizes this connection between God's creation and His attributes: "For since the creation of the world God's invisible qualities—his eternal power and divine nature—have been clearly seen, being understood from what has been made, so that people are without excuse."

In the embrace of nature's awe-inspiring landscapes, one often finds a sense of serenity that echoes the Creator's peaceful essence. These moments become sacred encounters, where the Creator's peace permeates the very fabric of existence, offering solace and reaffirming His everlasting presence.

This personal journey to inner peace with God is a tapestry woven from diverse threads of experiences—a mosaic of trials, reflections, and encounters with the divine. It's in these moments that believers discover the profound truth echoed in Philippians 4:7: "And the peace of God, which transcends all understanding, will guard your hearts and your minds in Christ Jesus." This peace, found through personal revelations, becomes an unwavering anchor, guarding hearts and minds in the midst of life's ebb and flow.

GOD'S PEACE:

A STRONGHOLD IN HARD TIMES

One of the most profound truths about God's peace is its unwavering presence, especially in the face of life's most challenging moments. It's not merely a fleeting emotion that vanishes amidst turmoil; instead, it stands as an unshakable fortress, a stronghold for our souls. God's peace isn't intimidated by the storms but rather becomes the anchor that steadies us amid turbulent seas.

This assurance doesn't imply that trials won't come, but it guarantees that in the midst of these trials, God's peace remains a steadfast companion. It's a reassurance that these storms aren't indicators of His absence but opportunities for His intervention and revelation of His sustaining grace.

Jesus, in His promise found in John 14:27, bequeaths a legacy of peace to His followers: "Peace I leave with you; my peace I give you. I do not give to you as the world gives. Do not let your hearts be troubled and do not be afraid." Here, He bestows a peace that transcends worldly understanding—a peace that isn't contingent upon favorable circumstances but rooted in His enduring presence.

This divine peace doesn't exempt us from adversity; rather, it equips us with strength and courage to confront challenges head-on. It's an assurance that our security doesn't hinge on the ever-changing circumstances but is firmly anchored in the unchanging nature of our sovereign God.

The Apostle Paul echoes this sentiment in Romans 8:38-39, affirming the unwavering nature of God's love and its role in securing us amidst trials: "For I am convinced that neither death nor life, neither angels nor demons, neither the present nor the future, nor any powers, neither height nor depth, nor anything else in all creation, will be able to separate us from the love of God that is in Christ Jesus our Lord."

God's peace doesn't exempt us from the storms of life; instead, it fortifies our spirits, empowering us to navigate through the tempests with a steadfast trust in His unfailing presence. In the refuge of His peace, we find the strength to endure and the courage to face each trial, knowing that our souls are secured in His unshakeable embrace.

MENTAL PEACE THROUGH GOD THE ULTIMATE SOLACE

In the tumultuous landscape of life, where stressors and uncertainties loom large, mental peace becomes an invaluable treasure. Here, amidst the chaos, God's peace emerges as the ultimate solace and remedy.

God's peace operates as a divine therapy, unlike any other. It possesses a transformative power that transcends human understanding, offering solace that quiets our racing thoughts and eases the burdens of our anxieties. This serene tranquility isn't just a momentary respite; it's a profound state of being—a peace that surpasses the temporary offerings of the world.

The words of Jesus in John 14:27 resonate profoundly in this context: "Peace I leave with you; my peace I give you. I do not give to you as the world gives. Do not let your hearts be troubled and do not be afraid." Here, He presents a peace that isn't subject to the fluctuations of the world but endures as an unwavering anchor for our souls.

This divine peace liberates us from the clutter of the mind, providing a sanctuary where worries and fears find solace. It's an invitation to experience a tranquility that surpasses mere absence of turmoil—a peace that permeates every corner of our being and remains unshaken amidst life's storms.

Philippians 4:7 beautifully captures the essence of this divine peace: "And the peace of God, which transcends all understanding, will guard your hearts and your minds in Christ Jesus." It's a peace that stands guard over our minds, shielding us from the overwhelming anxieties of the world, and offering a serene refuge in the presence of God.

Embracing God's peace doesn't mean an absence of challenges, but rather it bestows us with a deep-seated calmness that empowers us to face these challenges with unwavering faith and strength. It's a peace that becomes our sanctuary, our anchor amidst life's tempests, reminding us that in God's presence, mental peace isn't just a fleeting moment—it's an enduring state of being.

GOD'S PEACE VS WORLD'S PEACE

A STARK CONTRAST

*G*od's peace stands in stark contrast to the superficial and fleeting peace offered by the world. Worldly peace often hinges on transient circumstances—an absence of conflict, temporary prosperity, or momentary pleasures. However, this peace is fragile, easily disrupted by the shifting sands of life's circumstances.

Contrastingly, God's peace is enduring and profound. It isn't tethered to external conditions but is anchored in the spiritual realm and nurtured through a personal relationship with the Creator. Jesus Himself emphasized this distinction in John 16:33: "I have told you these things, so that in me you may have peace. In this world, you will have trouble. But take heart! I have overcome the world." Here, He acknowledges the inevitability of trials in the world but assures us of His triumph, offering a peace that transcends worldly understanding.

The Apostle Paul underscores this contrast in Colossians 3:15: "Let the peace of Christ rule in your hearts since as members of one body you were called to peace. And be thankful." This peace isn't contingent upon external factors but flows from the spiritual realm, governing our hearts and uniting us in harmony with one another.

God's peace thrives in the midst of chaos, sustains us through trials, and flourishes within the depths of faith. It's a peace that sustains believers in all circumstances, as stated in Philippians 4:12-13: "I know what it is to be in need, and I know what it is to have plenty. I have learned the secret of being content in any and every situation, whether well fed or hungry, whether living in plenty or in want. I can do all this through him who gives me strength." This peace isn't dictated by external abundance or lack but finds its foundation in the unchanging strength of God.

In the intricate tapestry of life, while the world offers fleeting moments of peace, God's peace remains a constant—a transformative force that transcends the transient nature of the world, offering a deep and enduring tranquility to those who seek refuge in the Creator.

MAINTAINING GOD'S PEACE
SUSTAINING SPIRITUAL SERENITY

Maintaining God's peace is an ongoing journey that requires dedication and deliberate choices aligned with His principles. It encompasses various practices and a continuous focus on nurturing spiritual serenity.

Central to this endeavor is unwavering trust in God. Proverbs 3:5-6 encourages this trust: "Trust in the Lord with all your heart and lean not on your own understanding; in all your ways submit to him, and he will make your paths straight." This trust serves as the bedrock upon which God's peace flourishes, guiding our steps and reassuring our hearts.

Renewing our minds with God's promises becomes a crucial practice. Romans 12:2 emphasizes this transformation: "Do not conform to the pattern of this world but be transformed by the renewing of your mind. Then you will be able to test and approve what God's will is—his good, pleasing and perfect will." Regular immersion in Scripture and meditation on His Word helps align our thoughts with God's truth, fostering a mindset conducive to experiencing His peace.

Consistent engagement in spiritual disciplines, such as prayer, worship, and studying Scripture, is vital. Philippians 4:6-7 reinforces the significance of prayer: "Do not be anxious about anything, but in every situation, by prayer and petition, with thanksgiving, present your requests to God. And the peace of God, which transcends all understanding, will guard your hearts and your minds in Christ Jesus." These practices foster intimacy with God, cultivating an environment where His peace can flourish.

Living in accordance with God's righteous standards is pivotal in maintaining peace. Romans 12:18 urges us to pursue peace with others: "If it is possible, as far as it depends on you, live at peace with everyone." This aligns with the call to live in harmony with others, reflecting God's character in our interactions and striving for reconciliation when conflicts arise.

In the pursuit of maintaining peace—peace with God, within ourselves, and with others—we position ourselves to receive the blessings of God's perfect peace. Isaiah 26:3 assures us of this promise: "You will keep in perfect peace those whose minds are steadfast because they trust in you." This perfect peace becomes the fruit of our intentional pursuit of God and our commitment to live in accordance with His divine principles.

CHAPTER TWO

EXPERIENCING GOD'S INCOMPREHENSIBLE PEACE

*I*n the annals of history, across civilizations and epochs, humanity has sought a sanctuary from the tumultuous seas of existence. Amidst this perpetual quest, a timeless and resolute tranquility has echoed—an elusive yet palpable serenity that surpasses mortal understanding. Such tranquility, as described in Philippians 4:7, transcends the temporal and mundane. It isn't merely a transient respite from life's turbulence; it stands as an ineffable bastion, fortifying our spirits amid the tempests of existence.

From the ancient writings of sages to the sagas of historical upheavals, humanity's yearning for enduring peace has been a consistent refrain. The verse in Philippians illuminates this unyielding pursuit, offering a glimpse into a peace that defies the ebb and flow of earthly trials. It embodies a promise—a divine covenant—that surpasses the limits of mortal articulation, offering solace beyond the grasp of human rationale.

This divine peace isn't a recent revelation; it intertwines with the very fabric of human history. It echoes through the ancient Psalms, resonates in the exhortations of prophets, and culminates in the teachings of Jesus. Its essence pervades the narratives of civilizations past, offering a beacon of hope amid adversities.

In the echoes of Psalm 29:11, the assurance of strength and blessing resounds through the ages. It reverberates in the depths of Isaiah 26:3, promising steadfast peace to those anchored in unwavering trust. Such verses, intertwined with historical narratives and spiritual revelations, herald the presence of an enduring peace—a peace that stands resolute despite the storms of human existence.

This inexplicable peace, woven into the tapestry of human history, stands as a testament to a promise that transcends epochs. It isn't a fleeting concept but an eternal sanctuary—a haven offered by the divine, beckoning humanity across generations and civilizations. It is the unwavering assurance of a presence that surpasses mortal understanding, offering solace amidst life's ceaseless turmoil.

EMBRACING THE INEXPLICABLE

1. In the labyrinth of human comprehension, God's peace stands as an enigma—an ethereal tranquility that defies rational elucidation. It's like the gentle breeze whispering through the leaves, unseen yet profoundly felt. This divine peace, as referenced in Isaiah 26:3, transcends the grasp of human intellect, offering solace in the face of life's tumult.

Imagine a weary traveler navigating through a dense forest, surrounded by chaos and uncertainty. Suddenly, amidst the tangled paths, a serene glade emerges—a haven untouched by the surrounding disarray. Such is the inexplicable peace of God—an oasis of calmness amid life's convolutions.

This peace isn't a concept confined to scholarly dissertations; it's a tangible reality woven into the narratives of human existence. Picture the storms of history—nations clashing, empires rising and falling. In the midst of this tempest, there lies an unfathomable assurance—an anchor for the human soul in Psalm 29:11, promising strength and peace in the divine embrace.

In simpler tales, it's akin to a child finding solace in a tumultuous storm by clinging to a secure anchor. Similarly, God's peace, beyond human understanding, becomes an anchor for the soul amidst life's storms. Its essence is embedded in the scriptures, interwoven with narratives of triumphs, trials, and unwavering faith.

This inexplicable peace is an unwavering presence, beckoning humanity beyond the realms of comprehension. It's the divine hand reaching through the complexities of existence, offering a reassuring touch—a presence that soothes, anchors, and transcends the boundaries of human reason.

2. In the realms of our existence, a profound peace stands sentinel over the fortress of our inner selves. It acts as an unwavering guard, shielding the delicate intricacies of our thoughts, emotions, and spiritual core. This peace, articulated in Philippians 4:7, emerges as an impenetrable shield that deflects the arrows of doubt, fear, and turmoil, ensuring the sanctity of our hearts and minds within the protective embrace of Christ Jesus.

Consider a parable from an ancient land where a vigilant guardian watched over a kingdom's precious treasures. Just as this guardian protected the kingdom's riches from marauders, so does God's peace stand as an ever-vigilant sentinel, safeguarding the sanctity of our innermost selves from the assaults of life's uncertainties.

This biblical verse echoes through the corridors of human history, resonating as an eternal promise in narratives both ancient and modern. It's akin to a timeless story, passed down through generations, of a steadfast protector offering refuge amidst the storms of existence.

Much like the fortress walls sheltering a realm's inhabitants, this divine peace envelops us, fortifying our hearts and minds. It doesn't merely bestow fleeting moments of calmness; rather, it weaves an impenetrable shield around our very being, assuring a sanctuary that transcends comprehension.

In the rich tapestry of human experience, this peace is more than a distant promise; it's an ever-present guardian, offering a refuge—a sanctuary in which our hearts and minds find solace and resilience amid life's ceaseless tides.

3. In the pages of existence, an elusive yet tangible peace reveals itself—an enigmatic essence that surpasses human comprehension. This peace, articulated in Philippians 4:7, remains within the grasp of those seeking solace in Christ, inviting them to surrender their burdens and uncertainties to embrace the profound tranquility that God offers.

Imagine a humble traveler navigating a labyrinthine forest, seeking a hidden sanctuary. In a similar quest, humans seek a haven from life's storms, yearning for a peace that transcends everything known to man under the sun. Just as the traveler discovers an unexpected clearing offering respite, so do seekers find an accessible refuge in Christ, away from the tumultuous paths of human strife.

This biblical verse resonates as a beacon amid the narratives of human existence, weaving itself into tales that traverse time and cultures. It's akin to an age-old legend whispered through generations—a fabled sanctuary where burdens dissipate and tranquility reigns supreme.

Much like the forest's unexpected sanctuary, this divine peace presents itself to those willing to surrender their anxieties and uncertainties, embracing the profound solace God bestows. It isn't an unattainable dream but a tangible refuge, an offering to those seeking respite amidst life's chaos.

In the grand tapestry of human longing, this peace remains accessible to all who behold Christ, beckoning them to relinquish their burdens and trust in a tranquility that transcends understanding. It stands as an invitation—a call to surrender, finding solace and sanctuary in the profound peace that only God can impart.

SURRENDERING TO THE INEFFABLE

Imagine a sailor navigating treacherous waters, reliant on an unseen anchor that steadies the vessel amid turbulent waves. Similarly, God's peace serves as an imperceptible yet steadfast anchor amidst life's uncertainties. In the depths of turmoil, this peace becomes our unseen mooring, grounding us securely in the unwavering love and sovereignty of Christ.

Such is the nature of the peace spoken of in Ephesians 2:14a—a peace that acts as an unseen but unyielding anchor for our souls. It's a divine assurance that amidst life's tumult, we are firmly tethered to the unshakeable love and authority of Christ, ensuring that we don't drift aimlessly in the storms of existence.

The words of this verse resonate as a guiding beacon, offering reassurance in the face of life's adversities. They echo through the corridors of time, from ancient tales of guidance during tumultuous seas to modern narratives of finding stability amidst life's chaos.

This peace isn't just a fleeting comfort; it's an invisible force, an anchor grounding us in the unchanging love and sovereignty of Christ. It holds us steady, preventing us from being swept away by the storms, assuring us that even in the midst of life's uncertainties, we are securely held.

EMBRACING GOD'S UNFATHOMABLE GIFT

In the labyrinth of life, an enigmatic gift awaits—an unwavering peace that eludes human rationale. This divine offering, embedded in the essence of faith, transcends mortal comprehension. It's a beacon amidst life's tumult, guiding us through the labyrinthine uncertainties. Surrendering to this incomprehensible peace unveils a sanctuary within Christ Jesus, where hearts and minds discover their ultimate refuge.

This divine peace finds resonance in biblical narratives, where its essence illuminates timeless stories. Consider the tale of Noah, weathering the storm in an ark, finding peace amidst chaos—a testament to unwavering trust in divine providence. In the New Testament, Christ's calming of the tempest on the Sea of Galilee speaks volumes. The disciples, engulfed in fear, witnessed the authority that quelled the storm—revealing a peace that transcends nature's fury.

As we navigate life's complexities, may we embrace this divine gift, drawing from the wellsprings of biblical wisdom and stories to comprehend its profound essence. It beckons us to anchor our trust in the divine, finding solace in the midst of life's relentless waves. In this surrender lies the unfathomable peace that transcends the constraints of human comprehension—a resolute assurance found solely within the shelter of Christ's embrace.

CONCLUSION

CULTIVATING THE CULTURE OF PEACE

*E*mbracing God's peace amidst life's chaos indeed sets us apart in a world often characterized by turmoil. It invites us to elevate our perspective beyond the transient nature of circumstances and immerse ourselves in the enduring truths found in God's character and promises.

In the midst of life's storms, God's peace serves as an unshakable foundation. John 16:33 reinforces this assurance: "I have told you these things, so that in me you may have peace. In this world, you will have trouble. But take heart! I have overcome the world." This peace doesn't exempt us from trials but empowers us to face them with unwavering faith in the One who triumphs over all.

God's peace isn't merely an emotional state; it's a transformative force that shapes us into ambassadors of His peace. It's this divine peace that fortifies our spirits, emboldens our faith, and instills hope even in the midst of chaos. Romans 15:13 encapsulates this hope: "May the God of hope fill you with all joy and peace as you trust in him, so that you may overflow with hope by the power of the Holy Spirit."

Reflecting the psalmist's affirmation in Psalm 4:8, God's peace offers us rest and security amidst life's uncertainties. It becomes our refuge, allowing us to lay down our worries and fears, knowing we are held in the safety of His embrace.

Let us not only seek God's peace for ourselves but become conduits of this divine peace in a world yearning for tranquility. The blessing from Numbers 6:24-26 underscores our role in spreading God's peace: "The Lord bless you and keep you; the Lord make His face shine upon you and be gracious to you; The Lord turn His face toward you and give you peace."

As we share experiences of God's peace and the comforting verses that have upheld us in challenging times, we build a community that testifies to the enduring strength and solace found in God. Let's continue to seek, share, and savor the profound peace that only He can provide.

FAQs

Absolutely, here's a biblical perspective on each of the frequently asked questions regarding finding peace in God:

1. How can I experience God's peace in the midst of chaos?

Finding God's peace within you in the midst of chaos is a journey grounded in trust, prayer, and faith in His sovereignty.

1. Trust in God's promises: Philippians 4:6-7 urges us not to be anxious about anything but to present our requests to God with thanksgiving, and the peace of God, which surpasses all understanding, will guard our hearts and minds in Christ Jesus. Trusting in His promises fosters an atmosphere where His peace can abide, despite the chaos around us.

2. Prayer: Philippians 4:6 emphasizes the role of prayer in experiencing God's peace. Through prayer, we engage in intimate communion with God, laying our burdens before Him, and opening ourselves to His calming presence. It's in these moments of prayer that we invite His peace to permeate our hearts and minds.

3. Anchored faith in His sovereignty: Isaiah 26:3 encourages us to trust in the Lord always, for He is an everlasting rock. Anchoring our faith in God's sovereignty—the unchanging nature of His reign over all circumstances—provides a sturdy foundation even

in the midst of chaos. This steadfast trust in His control brings a sense of peace that transcends the chaos around us.

By trusting in God's promises, having a prayer life, and anchoring our faith in His sovereignty, we create an environment where His peace can dwell within us, regardless of the turmoil in our surroundings.

2. Does finding peace in God mean an absence of challenges or difficult situations?

Finding peace in God doesn't guarantee an absence of challenges or difficult situations. In fact, the Bible acknowledges the inevitability of trials in our lives.

1. Challenges are inevitable: John 16:33 states, "In this world, you will have trouble." Jesus Himself assures us that facing difficulties and challenges is a natural part of life. However, He follows this acknowledgment with a message of hope: "But take heart! I have overcome the world." Despite these challenges, He promises victory and His abiding presence to sustain us through them.

2. God's peace sustains us through challenges: Philippians 4:12-13 underscores this reality. The apostle Paul shares that he has learned the secret of being content in every situation, whether well-fed or hungry, living in plenty or in want. He attributes this ability to find contentment in all circumstances to the strength he receives from Christ who empowers him. This verse emphasizes that God's peace enables us to navigate through challenging situations, providing us with the strength to endure.

God's peace doesn't exempt us from challenges but empowers us to face them with resilience and faith. It's a peace that remains constant even in the midst of difficulties, allowing us to find contentment and strength regardless of our circumstances.

3. What practical steps can I take to cultivate God's peace in my life?

Cultivating God's peace in our lives involves practical steps that align with His principles and nurture a deeper connection with Him.

1. Renewing of your mind with God's Word: Romans 12:2 advises us not to conform to the patterns of this world but to be transformed by the renewing of our minds. Regularly immersing ourselves in Scripture allows God's truth to shape our thoughts, perspectives, and responses to life's challenges. It's through His Word that we gain wisdom, guidance, and a deeper understanding of His peace.

2. Pray without ceasing: 1 Thessalonians 5:17 encourages us to pray continually. Prayer serves as a direct line of communication with God, fostering intimacy with Him. Through prayer, we express our concerns, seek His guidance, and open ourselves to His peace that surpasses understanding (Philippians 4:6-7).

3. Living your Righteousness: Isaiah 32:17 speaks of the fruit of righteousness as peace and the effect of righteousness as quietness and trust forever. Living in alignment with God's righteous standards contributes to inner peace. Striving to lead a life that reflects His character fosters a sense of harmony within ourselves and with others.

By renewing our minds with God's Word, engaging in continual prayer, and pursuing righteousness, we create an environment where God's peace can flourish within us. These practices nurture a deeper connection with Him, fostering a state of tranquility that remains steadfast amidst life's uncertainties.

4. Is God's peace different from the temporary calmness the world offers?

God's peace stands in stark contrast to the temporary calmness the world offers. There are distinct differences between the two.

1. Surpasses worldly understanding: John 14:27 highlights that the peace Jesus gives isn't like the peace the world gives. It transcends the understanding of the world. God's peace isn't solely reliant on external circumstances or fleeting moments of calmness; it's rooted in a deep, enduring source that the world cannot replicate.

2. Provides enduring tranquility: Philippians 4:7 further emphasizes this distinction by stating that God's peace transcends all understanding and guards our hearts and minds. Unlike the fleeting peace the world provides, which is often tied to favorable circumstances or temporary relief, God's peace is unwavering and enduring. It stands firm even when situations are tumultuous.

God's peace is not merely a momentary respite from chaos. It's a profound, enduring tranquility that comes from a divine source—a peace that remains constant amidst life's trials and uncertainties. This peace, rooted in God's character and promises, becomes an unwavering anchor for our souls, regardless of the turbulence around us.

5. How can I trust in God's peace when facing overwhelming circumstances?

Trusting in God's peace during overwhelming circumstances involves anchoring oneself in His unchanging character and relying on His faithful promises.

1. Trust in the Lord's unwavering character: Proverbs 3:5-6 advises us to trust in the Lord with all our hearts and lean not on our understanding but to acknowledge Him in all our ways, and He will make our paths straight. Trusting in God's unchanging character, His wisdom, and His sovereignty enables us to surrender our concerns and uncertainties to Him, knowing that His ways surpass our understanding.

2. Rely on His promises, knowing He is faithful: Isaiah 41:10 reassures us of God's faithfulness and presence in challenging times: "So do not fear, for I am with you; do not be dismayed, for I am your God. I will strengthen you and help you; I will uphold you with my righteous right hand." Reminding ourselves of His promises, such as His presence, strength, and help, reinforces our trust in Him during overwhelming situations.

By leaning on the unwavering character of God and anchoring ourselves in His faithful promises, we cultivate a sense of trust and assurance in His peace. This trust serves as a firm foundation, enabling us to navigate through overwhelming circumstances with confidence and reliance on His unfailing support.

6. What role does prayer play in attaining and maintaining God's peace?

Prayer plays a significant role in both attaining and maintaining God's peace in our lives.

1. Fosters intimacy with God: Philippians 4:6 encourages us not to be anxious about anything but to present our requests to God with thanksgiving. Through prayer, we engage in intimate communion with God. It's in this intimate space that we share our concerns, desires, and struggles, fostering a deeper connection with Him.

2. Invites His peace to guard our hearts and minds: Philippians 4:7 beautifully illustrates the outcome of prayer. As we present our requests to God with thanksgiving, the peace of God, which surpasses all understanding, guards our hearts and minds in Christ Jesus. Prayer creates a space for God's peace to dwell within us, safeguarding our thoughts and emotions even amidst life's challenges.

Prayer becomes a channel through which we communicate with God, pouring out our hearts to Him, and allowing His peace to permeate our innermost being. It serves as a conduit for intimacy, allowing us to experience the comforting presence of God and the tranquility that only He can provide.

7. Can I still experience God's peace even if I struggle with doubt or fear?

Experiencing God's peace is not contingent on the absence of doubt or fear. In fact, God's peace becomes a comforting presence that surpasses our understanding, even in the midst of doubt or fear.

1. Surpasses understanding: Philippians 4:7 reassures us that God's peace transcends all understanding. This means that it's not dependent on our circumstances, emotions, or even our doubts and fears. It's a peace that is beyond human comprehension, anchoring us in times of uncertainty.

2. Overcoming doubt and fear through faith: Mark 5:36 encourages us to have faith in God's promises even when faced with fear or doubt. Jesus reassures a troubled father saying, "Don't be afraid; just believe." This suggests that while doubt and fear may exist, our faith in God's promises and His character helps us navigate through these emotions, ultimately leading us to experience His peace.

God's peace becomes a constant presence that accompanies us through our doubts and fears. It's not dependent on our emotions but on our faith in Him. As we trust in His promises and lean on His unfailing nature, His peace becomes an anchor that helps us overcome the turmoil of doubt and fear.

8. Does God's peace mean I'll never feel anxious or troubled?

God's peace doesn't guarantee a life free from anxiety or troubles. In fact, the Bible acknowledges the inevitability of challenges and turbulent moments.

1. Troubles are part of life: John 16:33 acknowledges that in this world, we will face troubles. This verse acknowledges the reality of life's challenges and the trials we encounter along the way. It's a reassurance that difficult times are an inevitable part of the human experience.

2. God's peace amid troubles: Philippians 4:6-7 encourages us not to be anxious about anything but to present our requests to God with thanksgiving, and the peace of God, which surpasses all understanding, will guard our hearts and minds in Christ Jesus. This illustrates that despite the presence of troubles, God's peace acts as a safeguard for our hearts and minds, providing comfort and assurance amid life's challenges.

Therefore, God's peace doesn't exempt us from facing anxious moments or troubles. Instead, it becomes a source of strength and solace that guards our hearts and minds, providing a sense of tranquility and assurance even in the midst of life's difficulties.

9. How can I recognize or discern God's peace in my life?

Recognizing God's peace in your life involves noticing the profound sense of contentment, security, and assurance that it brings, especially amidst life's uncertainties.

1. Contentment and security: Philippians 4:12-13 reveals that through Christ, Paul found contentment in every situation, whether in plenty or in need. This contentment stems from a deep-seated trust in God's provision and sovereignty. Psalm 4:8 echoes this sentiment, affirming that in peace, one can lie down and sleep securely, for it is the Lord who makes them dwell in safety.

2. Amid life's uncertainties: God's peace manifests as a sense of calmness and confidence that surpasses the unpredictability of life. It's a feeling of assurance that comes from trusting in God's unchanging character and His promises, regardless of the ever-changing circumstances.

Recognizing God's peace often involves observing an inner sense of serenity and confidence that isn't dependent on external factors. It's a deep-seated assurance that despite life's uncertainties, there is a steadfastness and security in God's presence and promises. This recognition can be experienced through a profound sense of contentment and an unshakable trust in God's faithfulness, even when everything around us seems uncertain.

10. Is God's peace something that only spiritual or religious people can experience?

The inclusivity of God's peace transcends boundaries, embracing people from all walks of life, irrespective of their spiritual or religious background. It reflects the boundless love and grace of

God, available to anyone who seeks Him earnestly.

God's invitation to experience His peace isn't limited to those within a specific religious framework. Instead, it extends to individuals exploring faith, questioning beliefs, or seeking spiritual fulfillment from various perspectives. This accessibility of God's peace speaks to the universality of His love and the depth of His desire for a relationship with every individual.

This inclusivity also acknowledges that people may come to seek God's peace through different paths. Some might approach through established religious practices, while others may seek in the quiet corners of their hearts, through philosophical inquiry, or through life experiences that stir a curiosity for something deeper.

God's peace becomes a haven for those weary of life's struggles, a comforting embrace for the troubled soul, and a source of strength for those navigating uncertainties, regardless of their spiritual background or religious beliefs. It stands as a testament to God's willingness to meet people wherever they are and offer them the solace, hope, and peace they seek.

APPENDIX

*H*ere are some appendices or additional resources that could complement the book "Embracing Tranquility: Discovering God's Peace Beyond Beliefs":

Appendix A: Guided Meditation Exercises
Explore our series of guided meditation practices (Books and Blogs) designed to help individuals experience with inner peace. These exercises encompass various techniques tailored to different preferences, aiding in fostering a deeper sense of tranquility.

Bible Verses:
- Psalm 46:10 - "Be still, and know that I am God."
- Philippians 4:8 - "Finally, brothers and sisters, whatever is true, whatever is noble, whatever is right, whatever is pure, whatever is lovely, whatever is admirable—if anything is excellent or praiseworthy—think about such things."

Appendix B: Reflection Journal Prompts
A collection of thought-provoking prompts to encourage personal reflection and introspection. These prompts are crafted to guide readers in contemplating their experiences, beliefs, and perceptions concerning peace and spirituality.

Bible Verses:
- Psalm 139:23-24 - "Search me, God, and know my heart; test me and know my anxious thoughts. See if there is any offensive way in me and lead me in the way everlasting."

- Proverbs 20:5 - "The purposes of a person's heart are deep waters, but one who has insight draws them out."

Appendix C: Recommended Reading List
A curated list of books, articles, and resources written by Alain Lea for further exploration. This collection covers diverse perspectives on peace, spirituality, and the intersection of faith and personal growth.

Bible Verses:
- Psalm 119:105 - "Your word is a lamp for my feet, a light on my path."
- 2 Timothy 3:16-17 - "All Scripture is God-breathed and is useful for teaching, rebuking, correcting and training in righteousness, so that the servant of God may be thoroughly equipped for every good work."

Books available for you right now: The Void 1&2, Heart to Heart, Freedom From Fears, What Now, Sacred Gaze...

Appendix D: Community and Online Resources
A compilation of community groups, forums, and support networks for individuals seeking a community to explore and discuss matters of faith, peace, and spirituality in an inclusive and supportive environment.

Contact us if you are interested to listen Live Podcast or Messages of the son of God Alain Lea with CIAN.

Bible Verses:
- Romans 12:4-5 - "For just as each of us has one body with many members, and these members do not all have the same function, so in Christ we, though many, form one body, and each member belongs to all the others."
- Hebrews 10:24-25 - "And let us consider how we may spur one another on toward love and good deeds, not giving up meeting

together, as some are in the habit of doing, but encouraging one another—and all the more as you see the Day approaching."

- Proverbs 4:7 - "The beginning of wisdom is this: Get wisdom. Though it cost all you have, get understanding."

- James 1:5 - "If any of you lacks wisdom, you should ask God, who gives generously to all without finding fault, and it will be given to you."

Appendix E: Scriptures and Verses on Peace

An index of key scriptures and verses that emphasize the theme of peace. This compilation offers readers a diverse collection of sacred texts highlighting the universal peace which is only available in God, in Christ:

1. John 14:27 "Peace I leave with you; my peace I give you. I do not give to you as the world gives. Do not let your hearts be troubled and do not be afraid."

2. Isaiah 26:3 "You will keep in perfect peace those whose minds are steadfast, because they trust in you."

3. Philippians 4:6-7 "Do not be anxious about anything, but in every situation, by prayer and petition, with thanksgiving, present your requests to God. And the peace of God, which transcends all understanding, will guard your hearts and your minds in Christ Jesus."

4. Romans 15:13 "May the God of hope fill you with all joy and peace as you trust in him, so that you may overflow with hope by the power of the Holy Spirit."

5. Psalm 29:11 "The Lord gives strength to his people; the Lord blesses his people with peace."

6. Numbers 6:24-26 "The Lord bless you and keep you; the Lord make his face shine on you and be gracious to you; the Lord turn

his face toward you and give you peace."

7. James 3:18 "Peacemakers who sow in peace reap a harvest of righteousness."

8. Colossians 3:15 "Let the peace of Christ rule in your hearts, since as members of one body you were called to peace. And be thankful."

9. Psalm 4:8 "In peace I will lie down and sleep, for you alone, Lord, make me dwell in safety."

10. 1 Peter 5:7 "Cast all your anxiety on him because he cares for you."

Of course! Here are ten additional Scriptures and verses from the Bible that center around the theme of peace:

11. Matthew 5:9 "Blessed are the peacemakers, for they will be called children of God."

12. Psalm 85:8 "I will listen to what God the Lord says; he promises peace to his people, his faithful servants—but let them not turn to folly."

13. Proverbs 16:7 "When the Lord takes pleasure in anyone's way, he causes their enemies to make peace with them."

14. Ephesians 2:14 "For he himself is our peace, who has made the two groups one and has destroyed the barrier, the dividing wall of hostility."

15. Isaiah 32:17 "The fruit of that righteousness will be peace; its effect will be quietness and confidence forever."

16. 1 Corinthians 14:33 "For God is not a God of disorder but of peace—as in all the congregations of the Lord's people."

17. Hebrews 12:14 "Make every effort to live in peace with everyone and to be holy; without holiness, no one will see the Lord."

18. Philippians 4:9 "Whatever you have learned or received or heard from me, or seen in me—put it into practice. And the God of peace will be with you."

19. Galatians 5:22-23 "But the fruit of the Spirit is love, joy, peace, forbearance, kindness, goodness, faithfulness, gentleness, and self-control. Against such things, there is no law."

20. 2 Thessalonians 3:16 "Now may the Lord of peace himself give you peace at all times and in every way. The Lord be with all of you."

THE ULTIMATE INVITATION

Dear Father, in the freedom of your endless love and in the safety of your divine embrace, I acknowledge that Jesus Christ is your Eternal Son. I got lost in my own darkness, instead of living in your joy, I got crippled inside. Instead of receiving your love, my soul was disturbed. Today, I acknowledge and believe that the life of Jesus from His birth to His seating at the right hand of God was vicarious. I was co-crucified with Jesus, I co-died on the cross with Him; I was co-buried together with Him; on the third day I co-raised from among the dead with Him; I co-ascended on high with Jesus and I am co-seated at Your right hand with Him as well. I acknowledge in my heart and agree to the fact that Jesus Christ is Lord of all and over All!

I give myself in love to you today, just as you gave yourself in love for me and to me. Here I am Father, Jesus and Holy Spirit, LOVE me. Amen!

welcome back to your real senses!

The Father, the Son and Holy Spirit welcome you and celebrate your return [return to the right awareness regarding your origins and identity]. You are a partaker of the saving work and Life of Jesus Christ. The journey of love and discovery has started. It is important for you to continuously grow in the knowledge of the love, the person and finished work of Jesus Christ by allowing your soul to be fed with the words of grace. For you have been crucified with Christ, it is no longer you who live, but Christ lives in you. Therefore, the terms co-crucified and alive together with Christ defines you now. Christ in you and you in Him. It is a blessing to know that the life you live is entirely by the faith of another (Jesus Christ), so you have nothing to worry about from now on. He got your back from start to finish. Live your life overwhelmed by God's opinion of you.

I suggest seeking a community centered around Christ where believers gather to delve deeper into the teachings of Jesus, His Father, and the Holy Spirit. Through this, you'll uncover your true identity and realize the abundant blessings inherent in your union with God. Embrace and celebrate your place in God's family each day, honoring the richness of who you already are in His divine embrace.

You matter to God!

ABOUT THE AUTHOR

Alain Lea, a global ambassador of the Trinitarian Gospel, has traversed continents for over a decade, illuminating the world with the profound simplicity of the Gospel's Truth. As the esteemed Director of Christ in All Nations, Apostle Lea has mentored and equipped a multitude of ministers across the United States and worldwide. His disciples, scattered across the globe, ardently carry the divine message to millions seeking the revelation of God's sons.

An illustrious author, Alain Lea has penned an array of impactful books, from the enlightening "Sacred Gaze" to the thought-provoking volumes of "The Void 1 and 2," along with "What Now," "Freedom from Fears," and "Heart to Heart." His literary prowess, fused with an unparalleled understanding of the Gospel and the intricacies of human suffering, has inspired his diverse collection of literary works.

Throughout his dedicated service to the Lord and humanity, Alain Lea has meticulously crafted an extensive array of teaching materials spanning print, audio, and video formats. His ministry fervently distributes these invaluable resources free of charge, catering to the spiritual hunger of those in search of God's boundless love.

For inquiries and connections, Alain Lea welcomes contact at infos@christinallnations.org, perpetually driven by his unwavering commitment to share God's love and wisdom with the world.

www.ingramcontent.com/pod-product-compliance
Lightning Source LLC
Chambersburg PA
CBHW061810070526
44586CB00024B/2798